ESKRIMA STREET DEFENSE

ESKRIMA STREET DEFENSE

PRACTICAL TECHNIQUES FOR DANGEROUS SITUATIONS

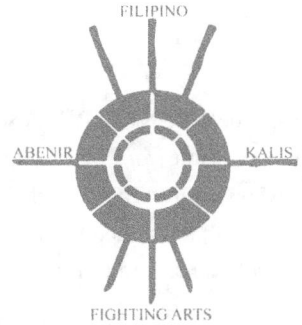

Fernando "Bong" Abenir

www.TambuliMedia.com
Spring House, PA USA

DISCLAIMER

The author and publisher of this book are NOT RESPONSIBLE in any manner whatsoever for any injury that may result from practicing the techniques and/or following the instructions given within. Since the physical activities described herein may be too strenuous in nature for some readers to engage in safely, it is essential that a physician be consulted prior to training.

First Published September 15, 2014 by Tambuli Media
Copyright @ 2014 by Fernando "Bong" Abenir

ISBN-10: 1-943155-01-1
ISBN-13: 978-1-943155-01-9
Library of Congress Control Number: 2015935665

All Rights Reserved. No part of this publication may be reproduced or utilized in any form or by any means, electronic or mechanical, including photocopying, recording, or by any information storage and retrieval system, without prior written permission from the Publisher or Author.

Edited by Mark V. Wiley
Designed by Summer Bonne

TABLE OF CONTENTS

Foreword 1

Author's Preface 3

PART 1: DEFINITIONS, PRINCIPLES, STRATEGIES 5

    Chapter 1: History and Definition of Filipino Martial Arts 7

    Chapter 2: The Abenir Kalis System 13

    Chapter 3: Preliminaries 17

    Chapter 4: Be Safe in the City 21

PART 2: ESKRIMA STREET DEFENSE 31

    Chapter 5: Hand vs. Hand Techniques 33

    Chapter 6: Hand vs. Knife Techniques 55

    Chapter 7: Hand vs. Bolo Techniques 77

    Chapter 8: Knife vs. Knife Techniques 89

    Chapter 9: Bolo vs. Bolo Techniques 101

    Chapter 10: Improvised Weapon Techniques 113

Conclusion 127

About The Author 129

FOREWORD

Over the last 30 years I have met many of the old-timers and new-comers in the Filipino martial arts society. Among the new crop of teachers making their mark is Fernando Abenir. Known as "Bong" to his friends and colleagues, Abenir has been building his name in the Philippines through his teachings at various locations, articles in the *Manila Times* newspaper, appearances on various local television shows demonstrating his art, and worldwide on Facebook and YouTube. His movements are representative of the combat efficacy of the late and legendary Antonio "Tatang" Ilustrisimo, and his late students Grandmaster Antonio Diego and Maestro Pedro Reyes, but with a hint of silat and other arts thrown in the mix. Abenir himself was a student of Reyes and Diego, among other known teachers in Manila. Impressed with his basic approach to the art, I reached out to Bong to see if he'd be interested in writing a book on Eskrima for use on the street—as opposed to its practice as cultural art form, spiritual tradition, or modern combat sport.

He immediately said yes, and together we spent half a year working remotely to bring together for you this book, *Eskrima Street Defense*. In my capacity as publisher I decided on the format and Bong, as the subject matter expert, decided on the techniques. And while the book offers a few chapters on the history, development and terminology of Eskrima—as it is seen in the Philippines—he then offers discussion on tactics and strategies for using the art in street defense and how to become aware of yourself and others in common surroundings. Self-defense, after all, is about more than defensive tactics; it is also about avoiding confrontation through awareness.

Eskrima Street Defense offers dozens of practical techniques for dangerous street encounters divided into six chapters: 1) Hand vs. Hand, 2) Hand vs. Knife, 3) Hand vs. Bolo, 4) Knife vs. Knife, 5) Bolo vs. Bolo, and 6) Improvised Weapons. These techniques are backed up with 20 key principles for application, discussion of the 10 most vulnerable points to strike on the body, how to become aware of your surroundings in the most common public spaces where attacks often occur, and a discussion on common sense rules for self-defense that everyone should heed.

Among Bong Abenir's principles are "Run if you must, fight if you must, but whatever you do, do it decisively and quickly," and "Attack, attack, attack until the assailant ceases to be a threat to your safety." Such concepts are often glossed over in classes teaching the art of Eskrima. This book, like street defense in general, is short and sweet and too the point. The focus is on safety, awareness, and how to survive on the street when you suddenly find yourself in a bad situation.

—Dr. Mark Wiley
Publisher, Tambuli Media
September 23, 2014

AUTHOR'S PREFACE

Eskrima Street Defense is a compilation of techniques strictly based on the practical application of the Filipino martial arts within the context of a street fight. Now what I mean by a "street fight" is when someone finds themselves in a situation wherein they must defend themselves or help another person against an attack on the street. It has nothing to do with the art or the sport of Eskrima; but rather its application in what are potentially life and death situations. Although there have been many books written about martial arts and self-protection, only a few of them feature the practicality of Eskrima when facing single and multiple attackers, both armed and unarmed.

In response to that need, *Eskrima Street Defense* focuses on different scenarios that may happen outside the safety walls of the martial arts training hall and definitely beyond the realm of sport competition. It provides the reader with different strategies, techniques and street smart moves that may help them out of a bad situation—and may even save them and others from serious injury or even death at the hands of a ruthless attacker. This book addresses how to translate the art of Eskrima to street-ready empty-hand skills against dangerous knife threats, against difficult situations which include third-party protection, against a bolo or machete attack, against improvised weapons such as broken bottles, steel pipes, an ice pick, and more.

Eskrima Street Defense also shows Eskrima techniques used in special armed situations, such as knife against knife encounters, bolo against bolo situations, blunt weapons against edged weapons and vise-versa, scarf against edged weapons, situations against multiple attackers and other possible street scenarios. Although no book can replace an actual training program taught by a qualified Filipino martial arts instructor, it is still a great guide for any individual who wants to learn a technique or two that might help them against situations where one's life is at stake. This book also serves as an added training resource for advanced FMA practitioners and instructors in any martial art.

I do, however, strongly advise those who are just starting their quest or pursuit in learning self-protection or in studying the Filipino martial arts that they look for a qualified instructor in order to deepen their understanding of the principles, concepts and techniques described and shown in this book.

This book was not created alone. I would like to thank my student Mr. Adrian Manangan for shooting all of the technique sequence photographs. Thanks to Abenir Kalis instructors Richard Grimaldo, Jong Rivero, Michael Cruz, Norman Manalili, and Leo Beltran; to Abenir Kalis Mandaluyong students Angel Fajutagana, Jay Habuhab, John Mark Marcelo, Bhon Corpuz, and Ms. Jam Chari Nuñez. Special thanks to Abenir Kalis Pinaglabanan Brotherhood for their support: Bryan Dy, Marc Tiong, Audey Joves, Dennis Eala, Thirdy Nabon,g Jonna Bee; and Abenir Kalis Philippines headed by the following Instructors: Herbert Panganiban, Luis Beltran, Chris Dalida, Marvin Mendoza, Abel Diaz, and Ronel Viñas. Last but not least, I offer a very special thank you to Guro Rommel Ramirez who has been my long time training partner who endured a lot of bruises and pain with me during our live sparring sessions and demos. Pugay. Thank you Master Mark Wiley for encouraging me to write this book. Pugay po.

Fernando "Bong" Abenir
Manila, Philippines, 2014

PART 1
DEFINITIONS, PRINCIPLES, STRATEGIES

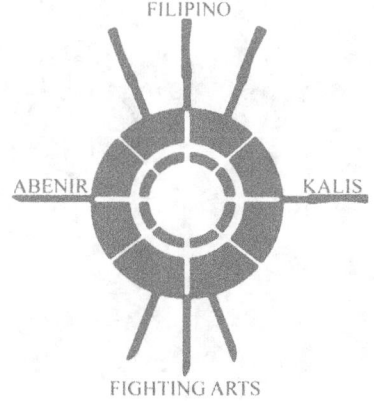

CHAPTER 1

HISTORY AND DEFINITION OF FILIPINO MARTIAL ARTS

© Artist Ian Sta. Maria

There are martial arts which have their origins in the Philippines. The practitioners of these Filipino martial arts (FMA) emphasize the use of blunt, projectile, and bladed weapons and hand-to-hand combat. Projectile weapons may refer to spears, bow and arrow, blow guns and knives.

Arnis is the popular term commonly used to refer to the Filipino martial arts in the Tagalog regions, especially in Manila where it is more identified as a stick fighting art.

Eskrima comes from the Spanish word *esgrima*, which means "fencing." In the Visayas, Eskrima is the common name primarily referring to blade-based Filipino martial art (though not always these days as the stick has come into more popular use).

By contrast, Kali is a relatively new term used here in the Philippines to refer to the Filipino martial arts, although it has been in use in the United States for several decades. Some masters have given their explanation as to the origin of this term. However, the word Kali is not a familiar term to most of the Filipino masters or even among the locals here in the Philippines, except among those who have adopted the name in the last decade or so. It is probably more popular in Negros through Grand Tuhon Leo Gaje of Pikiti Tirsia Kali, who is among those who popularized this term, especially in the United States.

On the other hand, *kalis* is a term which means "sword" and is now the preferred term used by Kalis Ilustrisimo Repeticion Orihinal (KIRO) headed

Eskrima Bolo Fighting

by the recently passed, Maestro Antonio Diego. He explained to us that the term is more appropriate for Antonio Ilustrisimo's art due to its blade-based orientation. Although its founder, Antonio "Tatang" Ilustrisimo, originally used the term Eskrima to refer to his art, it was at a time in the late 1980s when he switched to the use of Kali (Kali Ilustrisimo) due to its popular use among foreigners. With so many foreigners coming in to train and expecting to learn "Kali" (as opposed to Eskrima or Arnis), it was decided after Tatang passed away that the term Kalis Ilustrisimo ("Sword of Ilustrisimo") should be used in reference to his art.

I always keep in mind what the late Pedro Reyes from Kalis Ilustrisimo told me, "Names are there just for the sake of labeling the style and preserving the identity of the system. But It's how effective the principles behind every technique is applied during combat and how sound the philosophy of the art that truly matters." These days, all of these terms are being used to refer to all and any of the various Filipino martial arts, whether using weapons or the empty-hands.

A BRIEF HISTORY OF FMA

Nobody really knows the true origin of Arnis or Eskrims since there were no written documents on the art before the 20th century. This is probably due to the fact that most of the written documents of our ancestors were burned by the Spaniards and the art was outlawed by Spanish officials. As such, the practice of Filipino martial arts went underground and its masters and practitioners were reduced to roles as fight choreographers and actors on theatrical performances during Moro-Moro stage plays depicting combat between Christians and Muslims. Although for sure there was a martial art being used by our ancestors in order to protect them from other tribes, warring clans and foreign invaders. That is why we have the story between the fight from the army of Magellan and the legendary Lapu-Lapu and his warriors. Nobody knows exactly what kind of martial art they were using—or if they even had a name for it then—but it's quite clear that they knew how to fight well.

Eskrima Empty Hand Defense Against a Knife

As for the claim of others that Kali is the term used before Arnis and Eskrima, or that it is the "mother" of all Filipino martial arts, is still a matter of debate. But there is little proof of this in the records here in the Philippines, and thus it needs further investigation and proof before such a thing can be taken as true. However, there were references to Filipino arts by the likes of Jose Rizal when he studied Arnis as a young lad and even included it in his school curriculum when he set up one during his exile in Dapitan. We also have other well-known historical figures here in the Philippines, such as Juan and Antonio Luna and Marcelo H. del Pilar, who were known to have studied and practiced the art. An epic called *Florante at Laura* by Balagtas also mentions the term Arnis as a form of martial art. The term Kali, however, is not found in these records.

Today FMA is worldwide. We see Filipino martial arts featured in both local and international films, such as *Kamagong, Mano-Mano, The Bourne Identity* series, *Mission Impossible 3, The Hunted, The book of Eli* and many others. There are also a lot of instructional videos and numerous articles found on

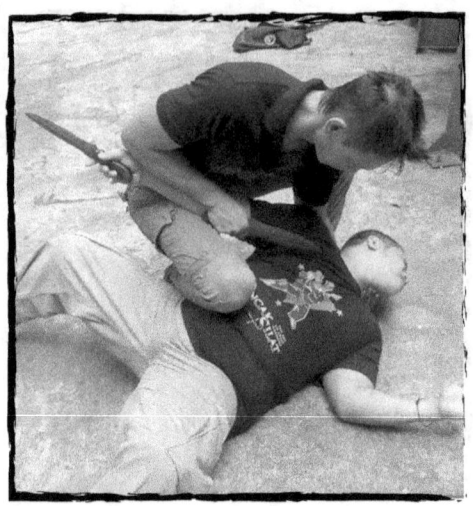

Eskrima Knife Fighting

the internet and books written about these arts. FMA have now become one of the most in-demand and popular martial arts in the United States and Europe. We must give thanks to the likes of Dan Inosanto, Antonio Diego, Mark Wiley, The Dog Brothers, Leo Gaje, Bobby Taboada, Edgar Sulite, Christopher Ricketts and others who have popularized the arts by exposing them to the public through seminars, instructional videos, magazines and books.

It should be noted that personal histories, or rather "stories," by many FMA masters and practitioners, are often made up and are not always trustworthy since most of the claims regarding the origin of their art are often shrouded in mysteries such as masters who dreamt of being taught by enchanted spirits, and others who traveled many treacherous mountains and learned their skills either through a beautiful blind princess or a hermit in a cave. These stories are quite amusing, but at the same time often ridiculous and unbelievable. Thanks to authors like Mark Wiley who have made a thorough investigation of the history of the Filipino martial arts that we have now a scholarly study of the subject. His book *Filipino Martial Culture* is a good reference that dispelled much of these "myths" surrounding the origin and development of FMA. We also have other good sources which come from Filipino authors and masters of the art like Rey Galang, the late Edgar Sulite among a few others.

WEAPONS AND TRAINING METHODS

There are many weapons and training methods used in the study and practice of Filipino martial arts. Here is a brief description of some of them.

Solo Baston, or single stick, is a form of fighting in which an eskrimador uses a stick measuring about 20-30 inches in length, with a diameter of an inch.

The free hand is used for parrying, striking and snatching the weapon away from the enemy.

Doble baston, or double sticks, refers to the use of wielding two equal length sticks. It is very beautiful to look at when performed by a skillful eskrimador. Another term for the movements used for wielding two sticks is called sinawali.

Espada y daga, or sword and dagger, is a form which uses a sword and a dagger and is assumed to have gotten its influence from Spanish sword play during the Spanish occupation of the Philippines. It is called punta y daga in Kalis Ilustrisimo, thus referring to the point of the sword which is used for thrusting and in coordination with the dagger as a secondary weapon.

Kutsilyo / baraw, or knife, is the form of using a knife for defense. The skills used by the Filipinos in wielding this weapon is highly regarded as a very practical and functional way of fighting with a knife. It also employs the handling of two knives. Abenir Kalis specializes in the use of a reverse grip hold of the knife, due to its stealthy nature, and is used in conjunction with punches, elbows, knees and kicks.

Mano-mano, or the empty hands, is a self-defense form which employs the use of punches, elbows, knees, kicks and grappling skills. Many do not know

Eskrima Espada y Daga Fighting

Eskrima Mano Mano Fighting

that this particular phase of Arnis, Escrima and Kali(s) is included in the curriculum; thinking instead that the art is purely weapons oriented. But the truth is that it is a complete fighting system where empty hand and weapons training are emphasized to help practitioners become well-rounded martial artists.

There are also fighting systems which are indigenous to the Philippines that do not emphasize the use of sticks or bladed weapons, such as Sikaran, Yaw-Yan, Dumog and others that are based solely on empty hand combat. Although they do have some training in weaponry, it is not their main focus.

The way of Filipino swordsmanship is geared towards combat efficiency and simplicity. But we practice it not with the concept of learning how to kill or to hurt people. We do this to promote our national identity and to inculcate love and respect for our country. It is also our means of expressing our human body through the movement and the ways of the sword to develop both physical strength and to sharpen our mental faculties. And we propagate this to preserve the beauty of our martial culture for the succeeding generations of Filipinos, including people from other nations.

CHAPTER 2

THE ABENIR KALIS SYSTEM

The Abenir Kalis system is primarily a blade based martial art which derives its bulk of techniques and fighting principles from the arts of Kalis Ilustrisimo, Yaw-Yan and Silat. The art's founder is this book's author, Maestro Bong Abenir, who has fused these systems in order to come up with his own training system. He has also added techniques and strategies discovered as effective during his live sparring. Most of the techniques that were effective during a full sparring session without protective gear were thoroughly observed by him, to see whether their efficiency was replicated many times and would, therefore, be included as part of the repertoire of Abenir Kalis techniques. Abenir believes that during a fight, wherein everything is sudden and happening so fast, that you may not have time to think but must instead rely on your quick reaction to respond to any attack or situation you are in. What's more, the empty hand fighting system could be practiced anytime at any stage or level of the practitioner.

The weapons progression is used in conjunction with the empty hand training progression in order for the practitioner to get a "complete education" in the variables possible with the major techniques and tactics employed in Filipino martial arts. The major characteristic of Abenir Kalis is efficiency. It is a very pragmatic and practical system. It does not waste time with unnecessary movements but instead goes right through the heart of the problem when dealing with an adversary. We make sure

that the practitioner is able to fight or defend himself in just a few sessions of training within the system. Although it does not mean achieving mastery of the skills and techniques within the system in such a short period of time but rather the skill and confidence during a street encounter is what we are after (learn to fight first, then work on the finer points of the art later). That is why we do a lot of live drills during the first sessions and help the student analyze the different strategies and tactics that could be employed during a street fight. It does not matter much how well you execute the techniques during a fight as long they hit the target. People are not concerned with how beautiful or skillful you employ your techniques but rather with who is left standing after the encounter. Only after learning this comes the formal training for the purpose of mastery and teaching of the system. This is based on the following principles.

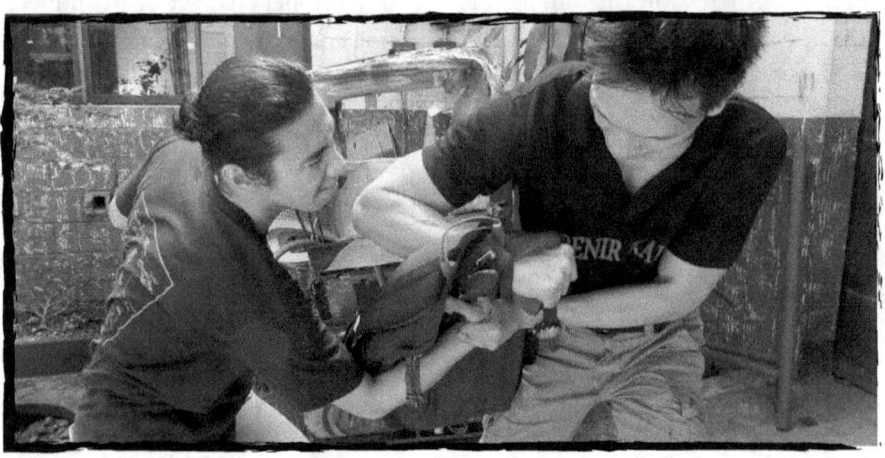

THE PRINCIPLES OF ABENIR KALIS

- Don't waste moves; be flexible.
- A parry which does not incorporate an attack is wasteful movement.
- A defense is an attack, an attack is a defense.
- Overwhelm your enemy with multiple attacks.
- Striking directly at the enemy's flesh is preferable to blocking the enemy's weapon.
- Your fighting position should be designed to make you a difficult target to hit.
- Don't be overconfident; be alert at all times.
- Be fiercer in your attack than your enemy.
- Be strong in your defense, and powerful in your offense.
- Move with speed and precision using correct distance against the enemy.
- The faster you hit the target, the better.
- Hit the nearest targets and those open to you.
- Attack when you see an opening.
- Employ your defensive skills when needed.
- Attack, attack, attack until the assailant ceases to be a threat to your safety.
- Hand techniques should correspond with footwork.
- Avoid wide movements in delivering your blows. Strike without telegraphing your attack.
- Wrist locks and disarming techniques are only incidental. A strike could cause a disarm that only counts as one beat which is faster and more practical to use than complicated locks during a heated encounter, especially against multiple opponents.
- Only engage in a fight if no other option of escape is possible.
- Run if you must, fight if you must, whatever you do, do it decisively and quickly.

CHAPTER 3

PRELIMINARIES

DIRECTLY SIMPLE AND SIMPLY DIRECT

If the objective is to learn the true art of Filipino Eskrima then everything should be done in a simple and direct manner in order to be truly combative and become very efficient in doing it. But the thing is, most people would rather study a system that has a lot of flowery and complicated movements. It's embedded in the human psyche to be drawn and be attracted to things that are seemingly magical rather than what is supposed to be real and natural. I sometimes also tend to do that but before I get lost in this state I would somehow awaken myself in order to get back to our system's true principle and philosophy. That is to approach combat the way we should. DIRECTLY SIMPLE and SIMPLY DIRECT.

ALIVENESS AND SPARRING

An old martial arts teacher told me that sparring is of no real value in actual combat because it has nothing much to do with what a thug or criminal would do in a real situation, and on and on he went trying to convince me of his

views. Well I never believed him and continued to be an advocate of what I refer to as "aliveness," which means that you go duke it out with your sparring partner and see what works and what fails during a quasi-combat encounter. That means that you get hit and he gets hit and both suddenly realize that you sometimes go home with a bruise here and there and it feels good. Although I believe that sparring is not the only tool you could use for practicing your skills, I really do believe it to be an essential part of martial arts training. Sparring teaches you a lot about timing, being able to read your opponent's mind and countering his attack, when and how to attack effectively, knowing and exploiting your opponent's strength and weaknesses and knowing yours as well. It also helps you to understand and feel pain when you get hit and what it means to fight under pressure.

I was once in U.P. Diliman with one of the instructors of AK Mr. Rommel Ramirez and we were there to demonstrate what our system was all about. Of course there were other groups too who were invited to demonstrate. I got so tired of seeing techniques being done over and over in a pre-arranged setting while everybody was intently watching these people. I really had nothing against them and I do respect their arts but when it comes to demonstrating what my system is all about then I would have to really show it. So after a few words of introduction I then instructed my friend to go live! Well we did stick sparring, knife sparring and hand to hand without any armor or protective gear and I got hit, my student got hit we were both getting black and blue lumps all over...... everybody was silent. We ended up laughing. That's ALIVENESS folks!

STICK AND KNIFE FIGHTING ARE DIFFERENT THINGS

I have heard a lot of old-timers in Filipino martial art circle says that learning how to use the stick will automatically give you the ability to translate it's techniques into knife work or whatever impact or edged weapon you are using. I do believe that there are similarities with the movements being used for each weapon but then again they also have their differences. And knowing this simple fact will give you an understanding of up to what point a certain weapon is effective and where its limitations lie. (Such knowledge could even save your life.)

Knowing how to wield a stick does not mean that you know how to wield a knife effectively. First of all a stick is an impact weapon, and the way you generate force in order to use it effectively as a weapon is very much different from a knife, which is designed to cut, thrust or hack. No amount of stick fighting would prepare a student for knife work. So the assumption that learning how to use a stick could be easily translated into knife work or vice versa is not true. Although the angles are the same and movement are similar, the law of physics when it comes to the use of different kinds of weapons says they are different. Try wielding a stick and a bolo or machete and you'll see what I mean.

A PLACE FOR LOCKS AND HOLDS

There are many reasons for learning joint manipulation techniques and strangle holds. They can be used as an effective self-defense method in some situations. They can be applied as restraints or arrest techniques when necessary. They can be useful in controlling or injuring a person to a certain degree and most of all they can serve as a bargaining position through which you could talk some sense to the other guy to stop whatever foolish thing he is attempting to do.

In my opinion, these techniques are actually incidental in nature which means they can only be applied when the opportunity presents itself. Never engage on a street fight looking for a lock or a strangle hold. What I mean is that they should not be used as your primary tool for self-defense. Hitting with a barrage of elbows, knees, eye jabs and kicks will serve you

better when it comes to a street fight, especially when dealing with multiple attackers. It would even be better to grab a hold onto something which could be used as a weapon or as an effective equalizer should the assailants be armed with knives or other things. Most real fights last less than 10 seconds. There is seldom an exchange of technique between combatants or what we refer to as fakes, feinting, trappings and other maneuvers that are only used as drills or those that are executed in study, sparring and tournaments.

As in almost all fights, the guy who lands the first telling blow is usually the one who wins. Against someone who is potentially dangerous and who constantly engages himself in trouble or does criminal acts as his way of living, it would be very risky to depend on locks and holds as your first line of defense. This is especially true if you are just a beginner in the martial arts because even for those who have achieved a high skill in the application of these techniques in the dojo it very difficult to apply these skills against a very aggressive opponent who happens to be punching, kicking, elbowing or even biting, simultaneously. It becomes even more difficult if you were up against two or more attackers. It would be like trying to catch three soccer balls in order to protect your goal. Forget what you see in the movies or even in the Ultimate Fighting Championship for that matter because we are talking about the real thing where everything is unrehearsed, goes without rules, no referees, no audience, no tap outs and no time limits. This is the world where guns, knives, broken bottles, tires and even trash cans can be used.

The best equation would be to hit-hit-hit then lock, if necessary, and not lock-lock-lock, then hit. Always remember that in most instances in street attacks, the prudent behavior is to escape as quickly as possible. If strikes such as head butts, knees and elbows are to be used, there is often no need to apply restraining techniques or strangle holds.

CHAPTER 4
BE SAFE IN THE CITY

In this chapter we are going to look at some of the possible dangers that may arise on the street and in public places and suggest effective ways to deal with these situations. One does not have to act paranoid by constantly eyeing every stranger; although, it is necessary to stay alert and to be prepared at all times.

LOCATIONAL DEFENSE ADVICE

Public Transportation

In the Philippines not many can afford to own cars because it is still considered a luxury. So it is quite common for people to wait and endure long lines in order to get a ride, not to mention the irritation that goes along with a fully loaded public transport. This is the situation where pickpockets and robbers thrive.

I once had an experience when I was riding a jeepney going to Sta. Ana and a fellow passenger (who turned out to be the pickpocket) sitting beside me started to put his hand in his pocket as if to get some money to pay for the fare. Suddenly I felt that he was leaning too much on my side so my instinct told me something was not right. I held on to my wallet and found that it was almost half way out of my pocket. Quickly I grabbed my wallet and looked at the guy and in an instant he jumped out from his seat and went on to ride a motorcycle that was tailing us. Apparently, he had someone with him who was ready to assist his escape after robbing passengers.

This example was given simply to illustrate how physical techniques may not be needed all the time. This is especially so when awareness is more needed, like at times when you're in a situation where everyone is packed like sardines inside a train (like the LRT during rush hour) and you find the next guy breathing down your neck, trying to rob you. This is a difficult situation because an escape route  may not be accessible and you may end up getting hurt since guys like this are usually accompanied by other men. So awareness and staying alert is what one needs to prevent this from happening. It is much wiser just to get off when you sense danger and take another ride.

Rest Rooms

The ladies room could potentially be a dangerous place especially when it's located at the far end of the mall or other building. It is better to be accompanied by another female companion when going inside these places. Males should also be aware because there may be potential attackers in the men's room ready to stick a knife at you when you are doing you're busy at the urinals. In short, stay alert!

Movie Theatres

When entering a movie theatre scan the area before taking a seat. Pause for a while with your back against a wall and let your eyes adjust to the darkness, then scan the whole area and look for rows where there are other moviegoers. Avoid isolated areas since these are the best spots for would-be criminals to hide. It is much safer to be with a friend or companion because this sometimes act as a deterrent against criminals who more often than not choose victims who are alone and situated in a vulnerable area.

Approaching Your Car

If you happen to own a vehicle, it is best to scan the place where you parked it for suspicious looking characters. If you sense potential danger look for a roving guard or a group of other people in the area and seek help. But if you

are caught off guard and put in a helpless situations, then by all means do whatever is necessary to defend yourself. Your car keys may prove to be handy in such situations as they can be used to poke the eye of the assailant or rake his face. This will buy you some time to run and seek safety and help.

Entering Your Home

Here in Manila there was an incident where the house of a movie actor was infiltrated by armed men who tried to rob him. Eventually, the situation was reversed when the actor was able to get hold of his gun and went after the robbers, killing one of them. The robbers entered the gates of his home by timing their assault when the maid was about to close the gate. This is a common tactic among robbers which requires perfect timing. In such a situation, gated home or not, be aware of your surroundings and check out places along the perimeter where potential attackers may lie in waiting. Exercise common sense by not letting strangers into your home. Ask for identification when accepting packages or mail. When in doubt, tell the delivery man to leave the package in front of the door or simply ask them to come back other day. Remember, even a tough guy can't do anything when a man is pointing a gun at him. So it is best to use your common sense to avoid such situations.

WOMEN'S SELF-DEFENSE

I have conducted many self-defense courses for women and as I began to progress into my teaching methodologies I become more convinced that the best way to teach women to defend themselves is to teach skills that are simple enough that even a child would be able to execute them. The concept is to impart only a few key moves that can be applied against different kinds of attacks, and which do not take a lot of time or skill to learn. Therefore, I probably threw out 80% of the techniques that I teach otherwise and streamlined everything; keeping only the simplest, most direct techniques wherein the most effective targets are selected in order to increase the chances of survival. High probability of success is what I'm after in such courses and not quantity of techniques. It is in my opinion that teaching too many techniques will only tend to confuse the brain, especially when under real stress. It will slow down the reaction time for it could take a while for the brain to assess a situation if it is overloaded with many types of responses to choose from.

A lot of instructors would not dare to admit this simple truth for they want to keep their students for a long time, which is understandable for it helps to pay the bills. But there are many interesting ways that we as instructors could keep them attending our class. And one way is to introduce unique drills and innovative ideas of doing things that would help continue to spark the student's interest each time. Another important aspect of training is intensity and proper physical contact. Women who attend such courses, if they are to be successful, will need to realize that martial arts involves physical contact. Some women (sometimes even men) just don't like the idea of a male partner grabbing her hand in order to learn how to escape from

the hold. They don't like the idea of another person grabbing her from the rear in order to learn how to escape from a bear hug. And it won't be of much benefit to them if they are partnered with another woman for it will cut down the sense of realism. Remember, most female abduction and harassment cases are done by men so it is logical  that they would have to overcome their fear and be able to react instinctively when confronted by men. So the safe way to do this is in the training center where everybody is treated with equal respect. If they come to learn how to defend themselves then they better decide wholeheartedly if they want to progress.

There is an adage that says, "You fight (or react) the way you train." So if a woman seeks instruction on how to defend herself against trouble makers then it is required of her to train just as hard as anyone else. In fact, I don't really make any distinctions in my class. For me there is no such thing as self-defense for women or self-defense for men. Only self-defense. And these courses are more direct and less complicated than the classes I teach to those wishing to learn the *art* of Eskrima.

COMMON SENSE RULES OF SELF-DEFENSE

Rule 1. Listen to your gut. Very often, when something is wrong you get to have a strange feeling about it. You may feel as if there are butterflies in your stomach or a big knot tied around your waist. This is an important warning sign that tells you to leave the place, to take an alternative route, to avoid a stranger, or simply to look for a crowded place to escape from danger. Many times our instinct (or gut) feels, it "knows," that there is danger lurking even before our mind does.

Rule 2. If you are confronted, and especially by an armed assailant or a group of gang members, do first what comes naturally—shout for help and run!

If no one helps you, or if you cannot run and escape, then do what you must to survive the encounter.

Rule 3. Don't look like an easy victim. A person like this sends out messages to potential assailants indicating that they would not defend themselves or are too scared to do anything if confronted. Don't walk around projecting an image of a person with low self-esteem or low self-confidence or you may potentially be setting yourself up as an easy target. Instead, you should project an image of confidence with your head held up as you walk the streets. This feeling of confidence should also manifest in the way you talk and move as it discourages would-be attackers making them think twice before they make a move.

Rule 4. Use good communication skills. The way you speak is an important part of any self-defense strategy. In a heated argument, a lot of fights could be avoided if one only talked calmly. If the other person keeps shouting at you, in return be confident but speak in a soft and calm manner. This may help in making the other person realize what an idiot he is trying to intimidate or provoke you when he gets the impression that you are not going to succumb to his threat.

Rule 5. If all your rhetoric fails you, the final option is to fight back. You have to be prepared to use physical techniques to enable you to escape alive in such situations. Whenever evade-and-escape is not possible, resort to using engage-and-escape to end the encounter.

VULNERABLE POINTS

There are various points on the human body that are vulnerable such that being struck with even a moderate amount of force would result in excruciating pain or even death in some cases. Martial artist are aware of the location of these points which help them to develop defenses to avoid being hit in these areas. It also serves them well by striking the assailants in these points in the interest of personal safety. Whenever physical confrontation occurs the most logical way to defend is to apply simple techniques that would easily connect to the assailant's vital areas. This would either slow him down or knock him off quickly in order to escape, control or terminate the fight as fast as possible.

Finger Jab to the Eyes

If the assailants is temporarily blinded, he will have a hard time trying to complete the assault against you. This particular offensive move can be applied effectively at punching or at trapping range.

Knee Strike to the Groin

This particular point of the male anatomy has been emphasized in many self-defense books due to its effective result. But many people, including some martial artist, tend to neglect guarding this area. So if the opening is there, send your knee hard and deep into the attacker's groin!

Elbow to the Bridge of the Nose

Even a slight pressure to the bridge of the nose could cause excruciating pain. Such a blow usually causes the nose to bleed and the eyes to water, which eventually blurs the assailant's vision.

Strike to the Windpipe with the Hand Edge

The function of the windpipe is to let air from the nasal area come in and enter the lungs to then be converted into energy. Hitting this area would cause choking that might lead to unconsciousness. At the least it will cause enough pain and discomfort to halt the attacker's advance.

Downward Elbow Thrust to the Kidney Area

Should the assailant tackle you by grabbing both of your legs this would expose his back and you could hit his kidney area effectively with your elbows. This area is vulnerable because it is not supported or protected by the skeletal bones or muscles.

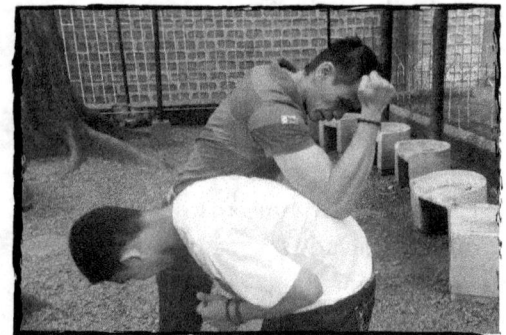

Heel Stomp to the Instep of the Foot

This is probably be most useful technique to break away from an assailants hold when either being held from behind or grabbed from the front.

Downward Thrust Heel Kick to the Kneecap

Although the patella or kneecap is not the easiest target to hit, it would easily put an assailant down and keep him in that position. According to some experts it would only take seven pounds of pressure to break the kneecap. So it is a target worthy of attention.

Elbow Strike to the Temple

A blow to the temple area could stun, render unconscious or even be fatal depending on the amount of force applied.

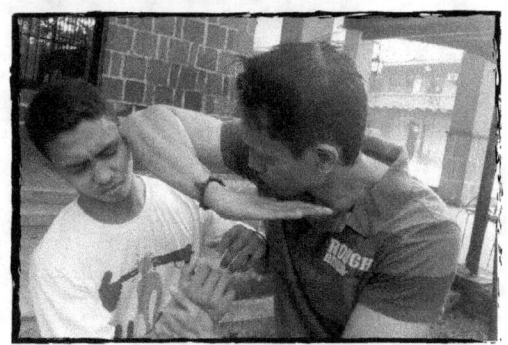

Knife Hand Strike to the Neck

Delivered forcefully, a blow with the side of the hand to the side of the neck could cut the flow of blood supply to the brain temporarily, thus causing loss of consciousness.

Knee Strike to the Floating Rib

The floating ribs are the ones at the very bottom near the waist. They are called floating because they are not connected to the spine, as the other ribs are. They just float there, connected only with cartilage, which makes them an easy target to break, cause pain, and halt an encounter.

PART 2
ESKRIMA STREET DEFENSE

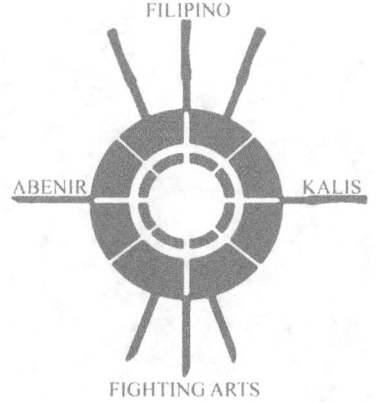

CHAPTER 5

HAND VS. HAND TECHNIQUES

"Only engage in a fight if no other option of escape is possible."

— *Maestro Bong Abenir*

Many street fights do happen without involving the use of weapons. And in my humble opinion is probably preferable than facing someone with a gun or a knife or any other deadly weapon because your chances of survival is much higher. But then again there are also reported incidents wherein deaths did occur as a result of a fist fight. So if there is a way for you to avoid an alt traction with someone then by all means try to do so.

Technique 1

DEFENSE AGAINST A REAR STRAIGHT PUNCH

Threat: The assailant grabs your shirt and is about to deliver a right rear straight punch to your face.

Response: 1) Simultaneously extend your left arm towards the assailant's bicep to stop the momentum of the punch and your right hand with your thumb sticking out to hit his eye. 2) Then grab his neck with your left hand and deliver a left knee to the groin. 3) And finish off by hooking your right arm around his left arm to maneuver him towards the ground.

Caution: Don't let your guard down. Raise your hands as a shield or a barrier that your attacker has to go through in order to connect his head shot.

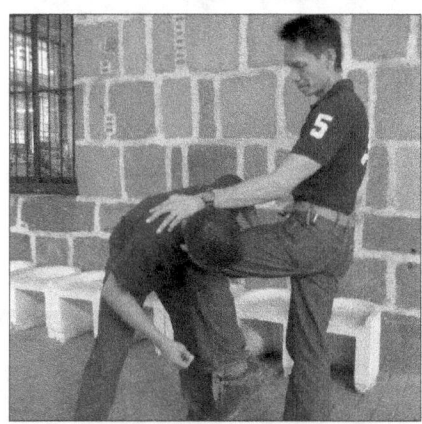

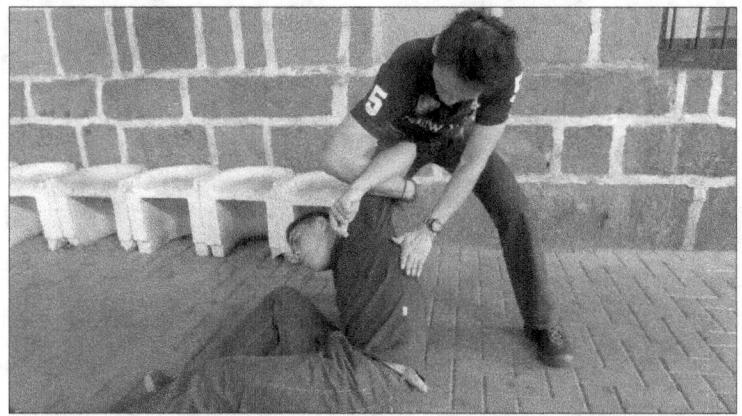

Hand vs. Hand Techniques

Technique 2

DEFENSE AGAINST A REAR HOOK PUNCH

Threat: The assailant tries to deliver a right hook punch to your face.

Response: 1) Duck under the punch while covering your chin with both hands. 2) Drive through with your left fist towards his liver. 3) Then grab his right ear and pull him down towards the ground.

Caution: Never forget to protect your chin. You might still get caught by his punch so it would be a good thing to have your fist protecting your chin to avoid getting struck directly, and possibly knocked out.

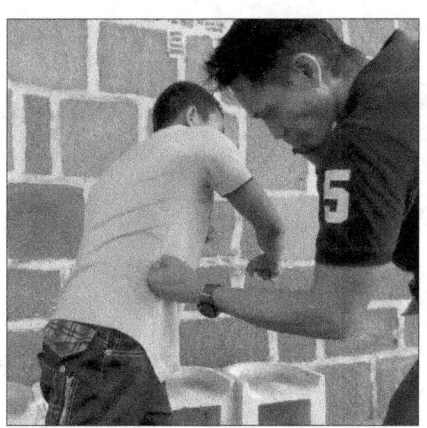
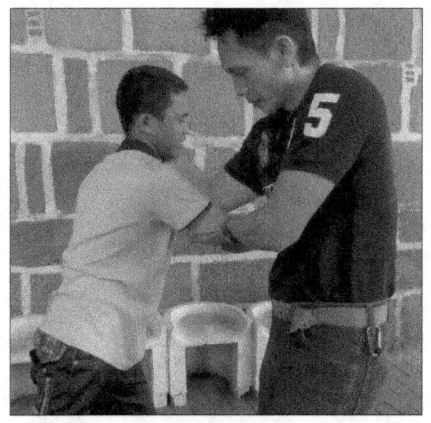

Technique 3

DEFENSE AGAINST A COLLAR GRAB

Threat: The assailant grabs the collar of your shirt with both hands.

Response: 1) Extend your left hand with your thumb sticking out to poke his eye. 2) Grab his groin with your right hand. 3) Push him down towards the ground.

Caution: Don't waste your time trying to twist his hand to break free. Hit him immediately.

Technique 4

DEFENSE AGAINST A REAR SHOULDER GRAB

Threat: An assailant grabs your right shoulder from behind

Response: 1) Immediately turn to the left with your hands both held high to put a good defensive cover in front of your face. 2) Then extend your left hand with your thumb sticking out in order to hit the assailant's eye. 3) Now go behind him to grab his hair with your right hand and pull him down to the ground.

Caution: Don't turn without raising your arms to protect your face or you might get sucker punched squarely in the face.

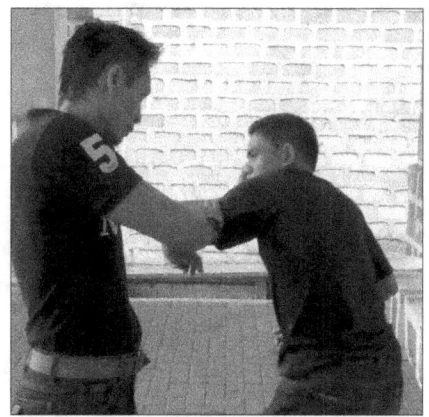

Technique 5

DEFENSE AGAINST A REAR-NAKED CHOKE

Threat: An assailant grabs your neck and tries to choke you from behind

Response: 1) Immediately grab his hand with your left and try to drop your weight down for stability. 2) Turn towards your right while tightly grabbing his hair with your hand while your forearm locks his hand as you turn. 3) Release your left hand to hook your fingers into his eye while driving him towards the ground.

Caution: React quickly as possible because a full bore neck choke is very difficult to break free from.

Technique 6

DEFENSE AGAINST A REAR PUNCH WHILE SEATED

Threat: An assailant attempts to sucker punch you while you're sitting.

Response: 1) Raise both hands to protect your face from the punch while moving your body to the side in order to slip the punch if it still manages to come through. 2) Immediately punch his groin with your right fist. 3) Immediately grab his head for control and slam him against any hard object

Caution: It's not easy to defend yourself from a seated position, so get up as quickly as possible!

Technique 7

DEFENSE AGAINST FRONT GROIN KICK

Threat: An assailant tries to kick you in the groin.

Response: 1) Sweep your right hand in a circular motion to the outside of the kicking leg, until his foot is caught in your hand. 2) Extend your left hand with your thumb sticking out to strike his eyes while you move toward him. 3) Close the gap while holding his foot and poking his eye, and place your right leg behind his support leg and push him off balance and to the ground.

Caution: Don't use force to block his kick with your hand. Use deflection and circular parries instead.

Hand vs. Hand Techniques

Technique 8

DEFENSE AGAINST A HEAD SLAM INTO A WALL

Threat: An assailant suddenly grabs your head an attempts to slam it against a wall

Response: 1) If you find yourself on a situation wherein your head is grabbed and about to hit the wall, raise your hands to decrease the impact. 2) As you recover, immediately use your hands to counter grab the assailant and jam both thumbs into his eyes. 3) Then use the opportunity to return the favor of slamming his face on the wall.

Caution: Don't sacrifice your head by letting your guard down. Use your hands to weaken the force of impact in this situation.

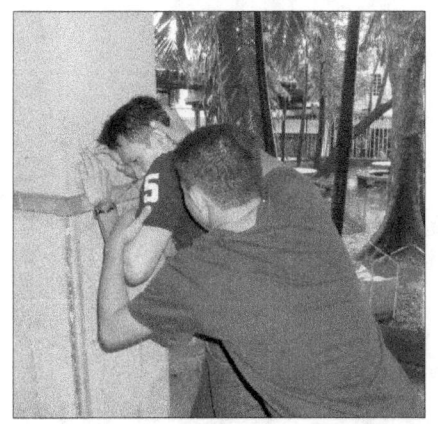
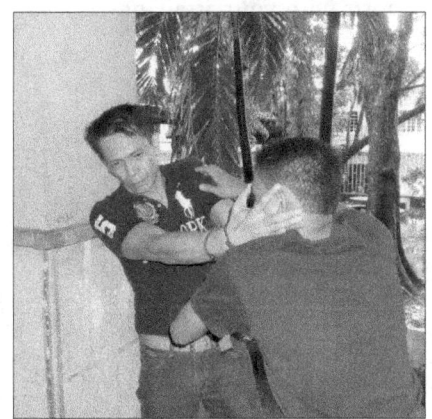
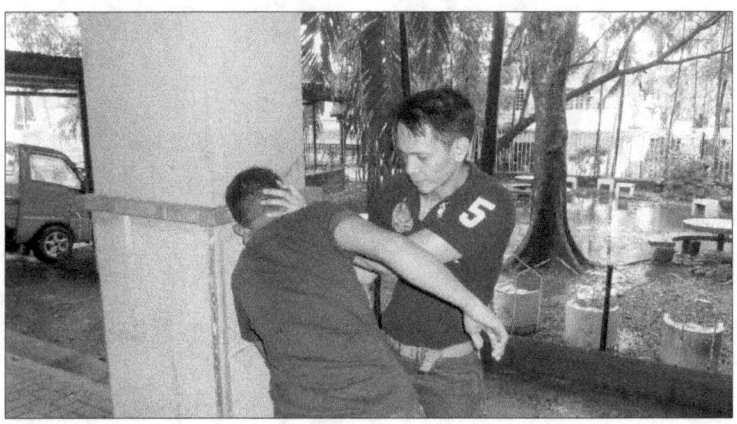

Technique 9

DEFENSE AGAINST TWO ASSAILANTS

Threat: You find yourself being grabbed by one assailant while another rushes toward you to punch you in the face.

Response: 1) Immediately grab the head of the attacker's right next to you and jam both thumbs into his eyes. 2) Use the first attacker's head to catch the other attacker's punch. 3) Then, as you violently push the attacker you are holding to the side, immediately kick the other in the groin.

Caution: Always use your peripheral vision to scan the scene if there are other cohorts with your assailant. Be aware.

Hand vs. Hand Techniques

Technique 10

DEFENSE AGAINST THREE ASSAILANTS

Threat: You're being held up by the arms by two assailants, while another is coming in to take you out with punches.

Response: 1) Use everything you've got to get out of this situation by kicking the attacker who rushes forward to punch you. 2) Then kicking upwards from behind with your left foot into the groin of the assailant on your left. 3) If you manage to get your left arm free after the groin strike, immediately grab the hair of the attacker on your right and slam his head to your knee as it strikes upward.

Caution: This is a very difficult situation. You must be alert at all times and look for an opportunity to line up the assailants to not get attacked all at once at the same time or find a wall against your back to make sure no one would be sneaking up on you from behind. But the best advice is to scan the area and look for the best exit way to avoid the situation.

Hand vs. Hand Techniques

CHAPTER 6
HAND VS. KNIFE TECHNIQUES

"Run if you must, fight if you must, whatever you do, do it decisively and quickly."

— *Maestro Bong Abenir*

A man called Mang Inyong shared with me his experiences in the many bloody encounters he had when he was young. He showed me all the stab and cut scars on his arms and the front and back of his body. I counted as many as 32! I began to suspect that he might be in some sort of illegal activities wherein deals had gone bad or that maybe he was really a trouble maker back then. But I learned a lot from him. He told me that there are certain people who get more terrified with the thought of getting stabbed with a knife than getting shot with a gun. I even learned that sometimes it is a very good strategy to play dead if you think that you're outnumbered by your

enemies. He told me about this one time when he was trying to get out of a very bad situation where more than three men were attacking him with ice picks and knives of all sorts until he went down on the wet ground (as it was raining heavily that night) and one of the assailants tried to make sure that he wasn't still breathing decided to choke him out by pressing the fingers on his throat which lasted for more than a minute that he was about to pass out. He had to play dead. He showed and taught me how to fight on the streets with a knife and also to use any weapon at hand in order to survive. I was around age 10 when I met him as I was already learning a little bit of martial arts from my father at that time. When we relocated to a new house in 1986, Mang Inyong was hired by my mom just for a day to clean our new home, which he gladly did. After that I never heard from him again. Remember that any fight involving weapons is the most dangerous of all situations. You'll never know what the result of the aftermath may be.

Technique 1

DEFENSE AGAINST A STOMACH THRUST

Threat: An assailant is about to thrust his knife into your stomach

Response: 1) Simultaneously grab the assailant's wrist with your right hand while your left forearm strikes his bicep, to create pain and also jam the momentum of the assailant's weapon arm. 2) Apply a figure four lock to apply tremendous pressure to break his hand. Note, the block and hit were before the lock. 3) Use the turn of your hip and sweeping motion of your left foot to put him on the ground.

Caution: Be sure to do this quickly and avoid your hair getting pulled by the assailant's free hand.

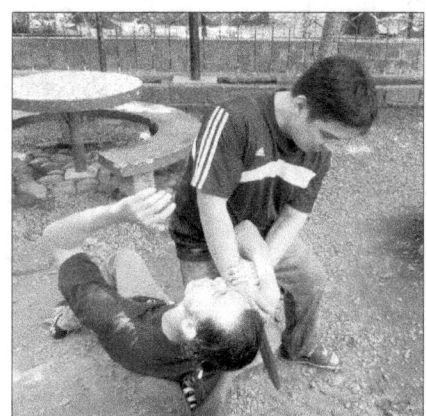
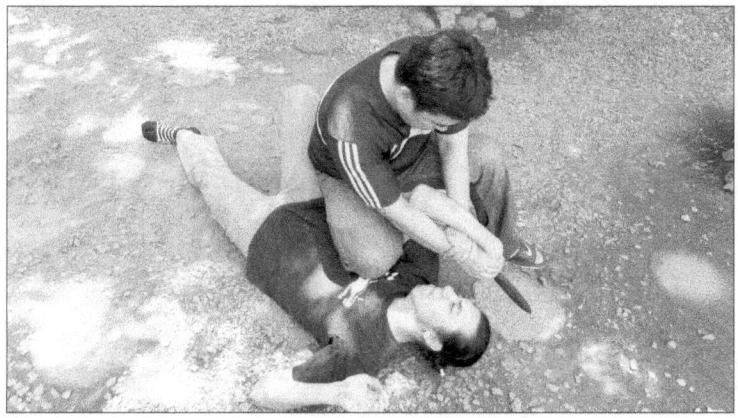

Technique 2

DEFENSE AGAINST A HOOKING KNIFE THRUST

Threat: a knife wielding assailant attacks you with a hooking motion aimed at your temple.

Response: 1) Immediately duck under the knife hook with both hand held up to protect your head. 2) As the knife passes over your head grab the assailant's weapon hand before it recovers and secure it tightly impeding its movement. 3) Grab the hair and hook your fingers into his eyes then slam his head to the ground.

Caution: I don't advise blocking the knife arm, as you might still get stabbed or poked at the temples with the blade's tip. But if you do, then be sure to jam the hand before it even starts its momentum.

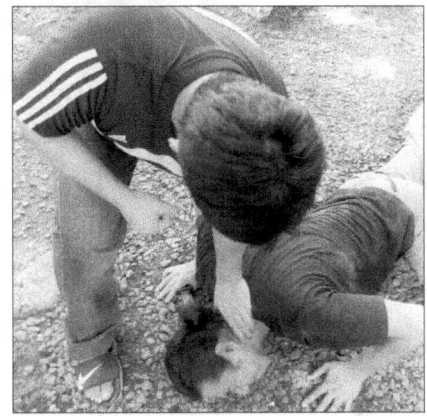

Technique 3

DEFENSE AGAINST AN UPPERCUT KNIFE THRUST

Threat: An assailant attempts to thrust his knife upward through your ribs into your heart.

Response: 1) Lean back and back pedal at the same time to avoid a direct stab. Be sure not to expose your chin as it might get caught during the knife's upward momentum. 2) Kick the assailant's groin violently to cause him excruciating pain. 3) If he reacts by bending his body forward due to the force of your kick, immediately grab his weapon hand and pull his hair and smash his head down onto concrete.

Caution: Blocking downwards is not the most effective defense against an uppercut thrust with a knife for it might still slip through your block and connect to your chin or neck.

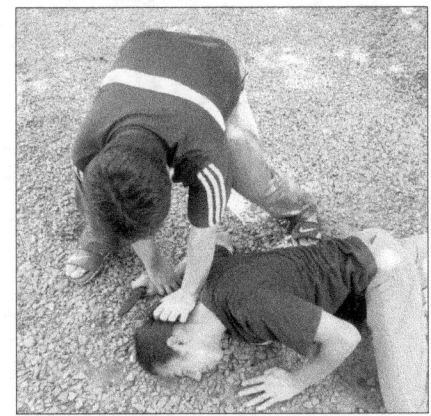

Hand vs. Knife Techniques

Technique 4

DEFENSE AGAINST A BACK HAND KNIFE SLASH

Threat: A backhand knife slash is coming at you. This might be the result the attacker's natural body mechanics right after delivering a forehand slash that either missed or connected.

Response: 1) Close the gap and jam his weapon hand with both of your hands. 2) Deliver a forceful knee strike to the assailant's groin then turn while maintaining a secure hold on his hand. 3) Then push his head with your left hand downward to smash his face on the ground.

Caution: Stay close to your assailant whenever you decide to go in. Don't create gaps that might allow him to slash or thrust you. Secure his hand tightly.

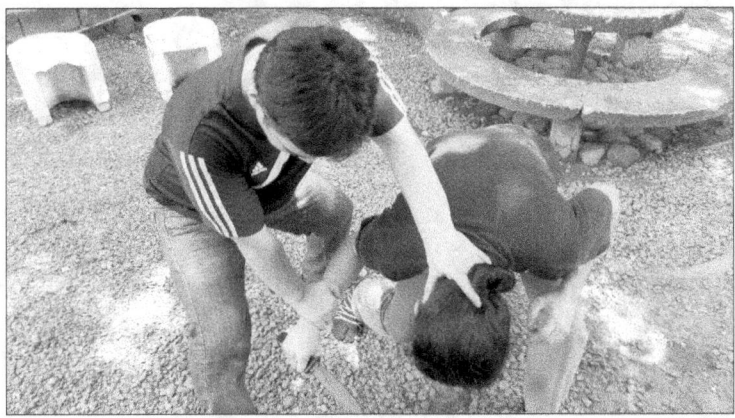

Technique 5

DEFENSE AGAINST BEING HELD FROM BEHIND WITH A KNIFE ON YOUR THROAT

Threat: An assailant holds you from behind with a knife pressed against your throat.

Response: 1) Grab tightly the opponent's weapon hand with both of your hands to prevent him from cutting your throat as you turn your body inwards. 2) Once you get free from his hold continue to secure your hold against his hand. 3) Then break is elbow by delivering a powerful strike with your right forearm.

Caution: Don't pull his hand away in the direction where his knife can slash you. Push it in the direction opposite of the potential slash.

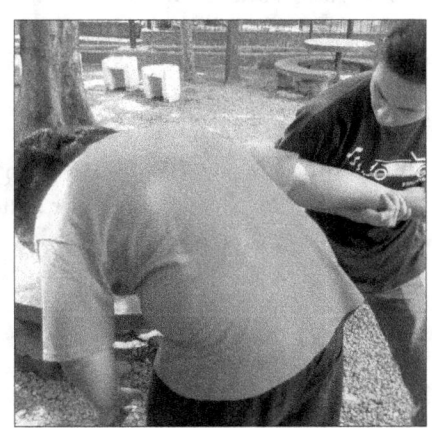

Technique 6

DEFENSE AGAINST A COLLAR GRAB WITH KNIFE ON YOUR THROAT

Threat: You are being held by an assailant pressing a knife against your throat.

Response: 1) In this situation the blade of the assailant's knife is held with the blunt side upward. This gives you a chance to place your left hand against the flat side of the blade with a downward force while your right strikes upward against his wrist, moving the knife in a controlled way away from you. 2) The opposing force may cause the knife to be disarmed, in which case you transfer it into your hand. 3) You may then use to against him.

Caution: If you happen to steal the knife away from your assailant, don't grab the knife using a full grip. Use a pinch grip method wherein you are holding the blade using only the tip of your four fingers with the blade resting on your palm while the thumb is resting on top of your pointer finger and not around the blade. Releasing your hand from this type of grip is easier should you decide to switch holds.

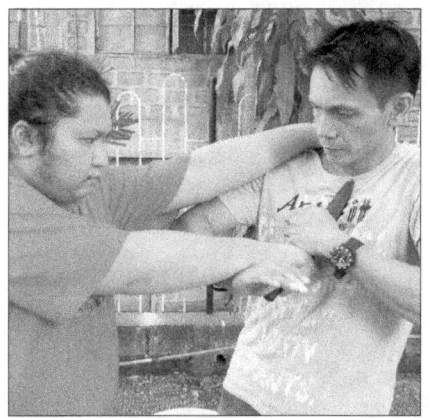

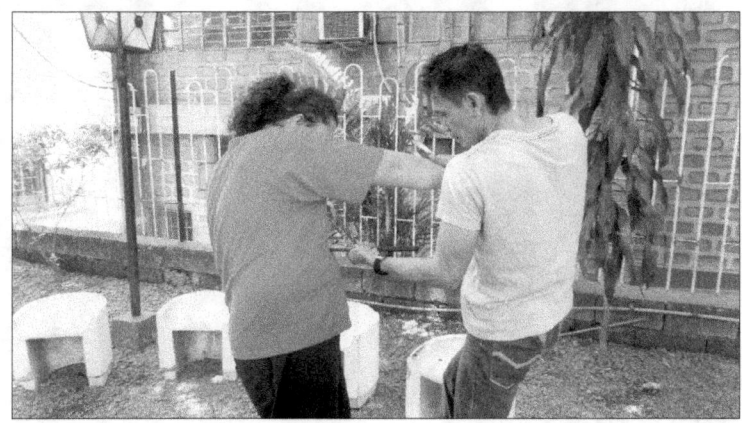

Hand vs. Knife Techniques

Technique 7

DEFENSE AGAINST BEING HELD FROM BEHIND WITH THE ASSAILANT'S KNIFE ON YOUR BACK

Threat: An assailant holds you from behind, pressing his knife against your kidney.

Response: 1) Quickly turn clockwise, using your elbow to push away the knife. 2) Your left hand grabs his wrist to impede his further movement. 3) You may use your momentum to thrust him with his own knife. Then pull out his hand and grab his arm to take him down.

Caution: Do this in a subtle but quick move. Don't give any signals that your assailant might feel with regards to your intended action.

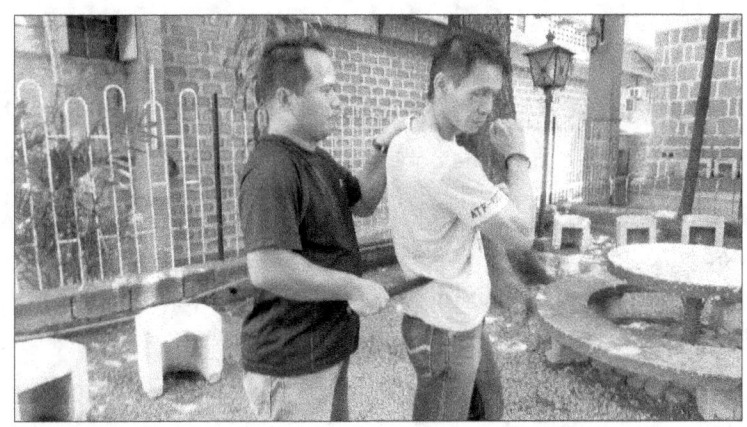

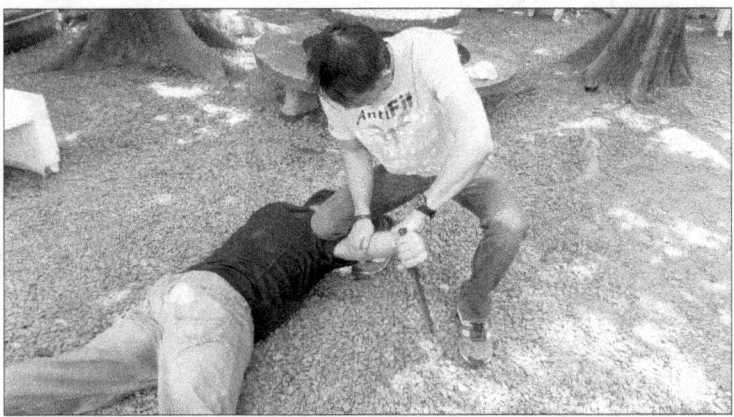

Technique 8

DEFENSE AGAINST A REVERSE HOLD BACKHAND KNIFE THRUST

Threat: An assailant is thrusting down on you with a reverse-hold knife grip.

Response: 1) Jam his weapon hand with your left hand to stop his strike then twist him wrist with a strong grip to off-balance him. 2) Immediately gouge his eye with the thumb of your right hand. 3) Then step behind his right lead leg with your right leg to off-balance him while slamming him to the ground.

Caution: Do this quickly in one move so as not to give your assailant time to use his knife to hook your hand, which could off-balance you and allow him to regain control.

Hand vs. Knife Techniques

Technique 9

DEFENSE AGAINST A REVERSE GRIP BACKHAND THRUST

Thereat: An assailant strikes you using a reverse grip hold of his knife

Response: 1) Jam the momentum of his hand using both of your hands, with your right grabbing his wrist while your left forearm breaks his elbow. 2) Do a figure-four lock by grabbing your right forearm with your left hand. 3) Quickly turn, using body momentum and weight to slam his head onto the ground.

Caution: Act on this quickly and avoid letting him hook your hand with his blade. Reverse hold knife attack methods are very hard to defend against especially in the hands of a knife fighter. Be very careful when dealing with it.

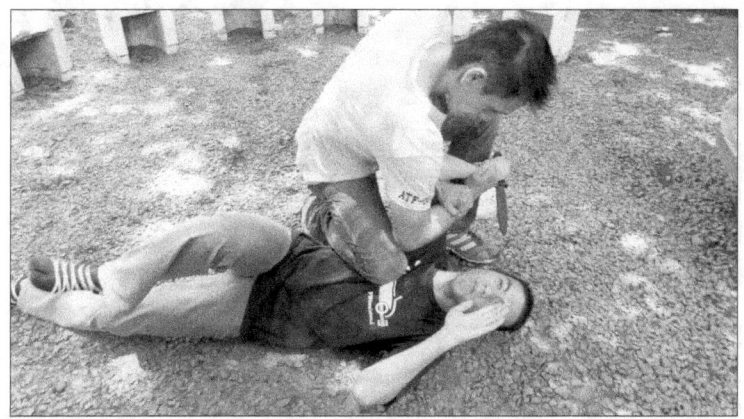

Technique 10

DEFENSE AGAINST TWO ATTACKERS, ONE HOLDING A KNIFE

Threat: You are by one who grabs you and is about to punch you while another is coming in with a knife to strike you.

Response: 1) Defensing again multiple opponents is extremely difficult. You may still defend by covering up with your right hand to block the punch of one assailant while simultaneously catching the other assailant's knife hand with your left hand. 2) Then redirect the force by turning to the side to control the knife wielding attacker, allowing him to collide with his partner. 3) Then grab the other's head as he gets off-balanced as a result of their collision.

Caution: This is a very difficult situation. Do everything it takes in order to survive such an assault. Beware of the person holding a knife. Never let him out of your sight as you deal with the other person who is unarmed.

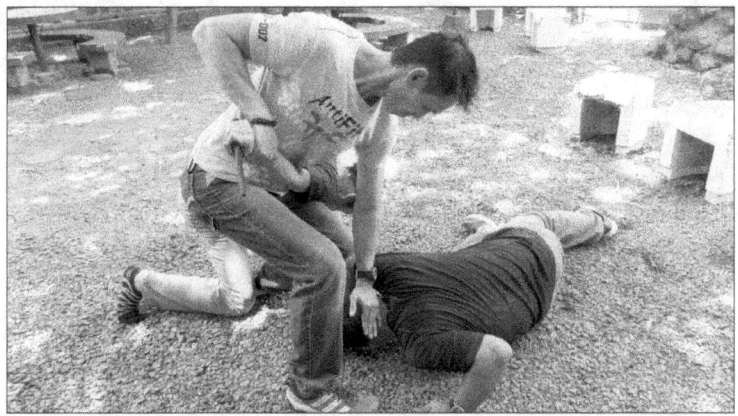

CHAPTER 7

HAND VS. BOLO TECHNIQUES

"Attack, attack, attack until the assailant ceases to become a threat to your safety."

– *Maestro Bong Abenir*

Unlike the knife or a hand gun, bolos are not commonly used by assailants on the streets due its size therefore very difficult to conceal. But there are incidents where this type of weapon was used to commit crimes. Here in the Philippines some reported cases wherein some men became a Jurementado and acted in rage wild like a mad man on the streets seeking vengeance and started hacking anyone who gets in his path using a bolo or any similar type of sword to commit indiscriminate acts of killing. If ever you happen to witness one in this mental state. I advise you to run.

Technique 1

DEFENSE AGAINST A BOLO NECK SLASH

Threat: An assailant attacks you with a bolo or machete directed towards your neck

Response: 1) Duck under the attack to let it pass over your head while parrying the back of the attacking hand with your left hand. 2) Immediately grab his weapon hand with your right hand to impede further movement. 3) Pull the weapon from his hand, pull his arm down to off balance him more, and finish with a knee strike to the groin.

Caution: Use ducking to avoid an attack that follows a horizontal angle. Never use this on a downward type of attack because it will surely hit you.

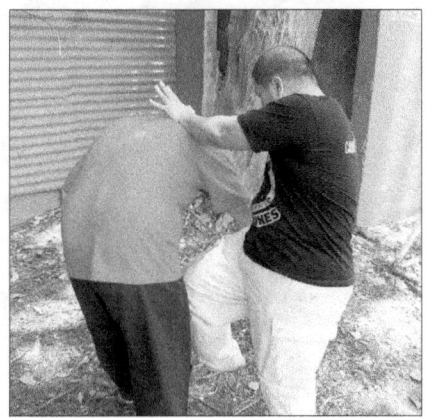

Technique 2

DEFENSE AGAINST A STOMACH BOLO THRUST

Threat: You are attacked by an assailant with a bolo aiming right through your stomach

Response: 1) Immediately step to the outside to let the weapon pass. 2) Then grab the weapon hand using your left hand and place your right forearm against the flat side of the blade. 3) Eject the weapon by pulling his wrist toward you and pushing your forearm toward him, and hit the assailant's groin right after.

Caution: Avoid just stepping back from a stomach thrust because the momentum of the attacker is moving forward and could catch you in its path. Side stepping is a safer way to evade this type of attack.

Hand vs. Bolo Techniques

Technique 3

DEFENSE AGAINST BACKHAND BOLO SLASH TO THE NECK

Threat: An assailant attempts to slash your neck with a backhand strike of his bolo

Response: 1) Duck under the attack. 2) As the blade passes over quickly get up and deliver an uppercut to the assailant's chin. 3) Take control of his weapon hand to ensure control of the situation.

Caution: Avoid back pedaling along the diagonal path of the attack because the tip of the weapon could still hit you.

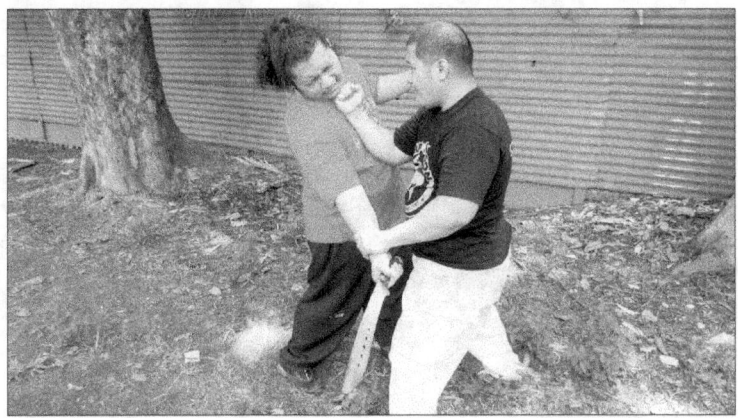

Hand vs. Bolo Techniques 83

Technique 4

DEFENSE AGAINST A BOLO SLASH TO THE BODY

Threat: An assailant strikes at you with a bolo using a horizontal slash aimed at your body

Response: 1) Pike your body while moving back to avoid the cut. 2) Immediately move forward to jam his weapon hand and place your right forearm on the flat side of the blade and rotate it to eject his weapon. 3) Grab his hand in a lock and force him to the ground to establish full control.

Caution: Don't use this if your back is against the wall for it will not give you enough space to avoid the cut. If you're in this kind of predicament it would be better to go forward and jam his weapon hand.

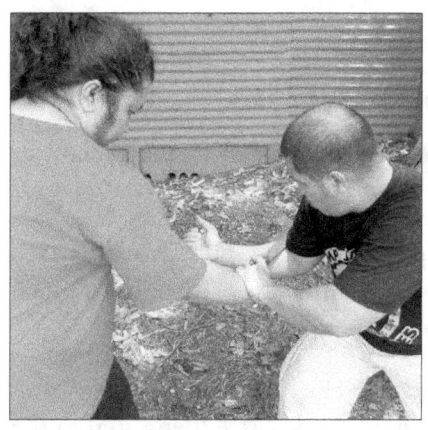

Hand vs. Bolo Techniques   85

Technique 5

DEFENSE AGAINST A DOWNWARD BOLO SLASH

Threat: An assailant attacks you with a direct downward forehand slash to your head

Response: 1) Rush forward to him using your left hand to deflect his attack and grab his wrist. 2) Jab his eyes with your right hand. 3) Then use a pinch grip hold to snatch the weapon away from him.

Caution: It is often very difficult to defend against this strike since it is on the center line. Back pedaling is not recommended. Use either a step to the side or deflection.

Hand vs. Bolo Techniques

CHAPTER 8

KNIFE VS. KNIFE TECHNIQUES

"Don't be overconfident, be alert at all times."

– *Maestro Bong Abenir*

I have heard some people claiming to be knife fighters just because they have studied some form of knife fighting art. But when you really begin to think about it, how could one become a knife fighter if that person has never fought with someone using this weapon? Can a boxer call himself a prize fighter without stepping inside the ring? Can a wrestler be called a professional wrestler without playing on the mats? Can you call yourself a stick fighter if you don't even spar against someone using live sticks? Real knife fighters are people like Mang Inyong and Tatang Antonio Ilustrisimo who fought and survived the grim realities of it. Knife fighting is a deadly art and there are

many stories of duels that did happen which either resulted in the death of one of the combatants or to the death of both. Even in depiction of movies, there is indeed a strange feeling when you see both people tearing, thrusting, and mutilating each other's guts out and destroying a life with a knife. So much commitment to violence is involved when that blade is inserted to someone's flesh with the hands getting bloody all over. I always say that knife to knife drills are amazing to watch, but the reality of a knife fight is grim.

Technique 1

COUNTER SLASH AND THRUST VS. FOREHAND NECK SLASH

Threat: You are facing an opponent in a knife to knife situation and he initiates an attack to your neck.

Response: 1) Use your left arm to block his weapon hand. 2) Immediately slash his bicep and thrust toward his heart. 3) Then step behind his lead leg with your right leg and take him to the ground for control.

Caution: Do not step back if you intend to block his hand because you will surely get your hand slashed if you do.

Knife vs. Knife Techniques

Technique 2

COUNTER SLASH AND THRUST VS. BACKHAND NECK SLASH

Threat: Your opponent misses his first shot with a forehand strike and quickly follows up with a backhand slash to your face.

Response: 1) Push his weapon hand away with your left hand as you cut his arm at the same time. 2) Immediately thrust toward his liver. 3) Then brace your left hand around his head and chin to control and take him down.

Caution: Don't wait for his third attempt to make a shot at you. Immediately get to him while he makes a second attempt after missing his first.

Knife vs. Knife Techniques

Technique 3

COUNTER THRUST VS. STOMACH TRUST

Threat: Your opponent thrusts his knife at your stomach

Response: 1) Parry his weapon hand to the side with your left hand. 2) Immediately counter with a thrust to his stomach. 3) Brace your arm around his head and chin to take him down.

Caution: Be sure to step to the side and not just rely on your hand parry to evade this attack. Creating more space between you and the weapon is safer.

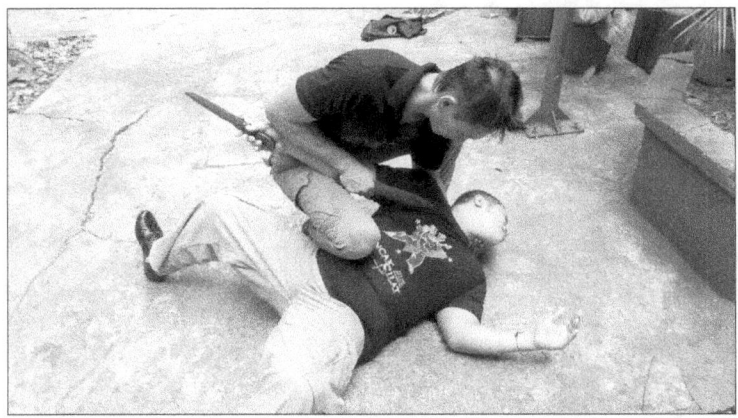

Technique 4

COUNTER SLASH AND THRUST VS. UPWARD FOREHAND SLASH

Threat: Your opponent delivers an upward forehand slash with his knife held in reverse grip.

Response: 1) Step to the left side and immediately cut his inner forearm while parrying his outside forearm. 2) Quickly move in to deliver a thrust to his body. 3) Then brace your hand around his head and chin to take him down.

Caution: Always check the weapon hand and prevent it from moving around your defense to attack you again by securing it as you go for a takedown.

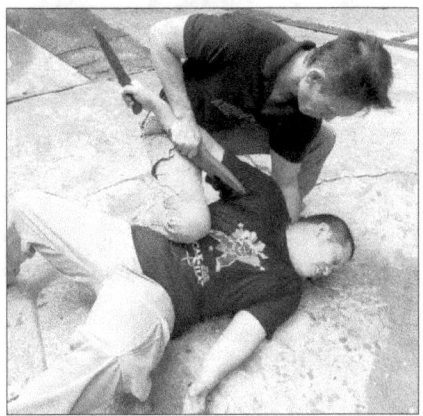

Technique 5

REVERSE HOLD COUNTER VS. REVERSE HOLD

Threat: Your opponent tries to slash you using a reverse grip with his knife

Response: 1) Step to the left side as the slash comes and deliver your own slash against the assailant's wrist or forearm. 2) Immediately follow up with a quick thrust to the kidney. 3) Finish by controlling his arm and talking him down to the ground.

Caution: Most knife handlers who use a revers grip hold may indicate that he is a skilled knife fighter. Therefore, be extra careful when facing this kind of situation.

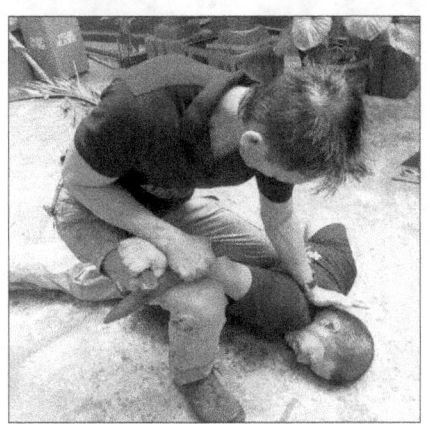

CHAPTER 9

BOLO VS. BOLO TECHNIQUES

"Run if you must, fight if you must; but whatever you do, do it decisively and quickly."

— *Maestro Bong Abenir*

The way of Filipino swordsmanship is geared toward combat efficiency and simplicity. But we practice it not with the concept of learning how to kill or to hurt people. We do this to promote our national identity and to inculcate love and respect for our country. It is also our means of expressing our human body through the movement and the ways of the sword to develop physical strength and to sharpen our mental faculties.

Technique 1

TECHNIQUE AGAINST A FOREHAND BOLO STRIKE

Threat: Your opponent delivers a horizontal attack at your neck with his bolo

Response: 1) Attack along the centerline in order to connect first with the tip of your blade, slashing the assailant's eyes. 2) Then maneuver your left hand over his attacking hand and let the flat side of your blade rest against his blade to protect your hand from getting cut. 3) Then in one swift motion push his weapon hand downward with your left hand while your blade slashes upward cutting the opponent's torso, and perhaps up to his neck.

Caution: Avoid executing this move too close to your body because you will surely absorb the full force of impact from the assailant's strike and this could destroy your defense in the process. Catch it just as his weapon passes mid-point, then execute the movement.

Bolo vs. Bolo Techniques 103

Technique 2

TECHNIQUE AGAINST A FOREHAND NECK STRIKE

Threat: Your opponent strikes at you with a diagonal downward forehand slash

Response: 1) Step to your left side with your left foot while also letting your right foot slide back a bit. 2) At the same time deliver a diagonal blow to the assailant's inner forearm. 3) Then step forward with your left foot to thrust him with your weapon.

Caution: Be sure to lean your body backward while stepping to the side as you avoid his cut.

Bolo vs. Bolo Techniques

Technique 3

TECHNIQUE AGAINST A DOWNWARD HEAD SLASH

Threat: Your opponent delivers a straight downward cut to your head with the intention of cleaving you in half.

Response: 1) Parry with your left hand while using the flat side of your blade to deflect his blade. 2) Immediately roll your blade around his to cut the assailant's neck while grabbing his weapon hand for control. 3) Continue to move by turning to your right to take him to the ground.

Caution: Be sure to step aside as you parry in order to deflect his attack effectively because executing your defense without proper footwork might fail.

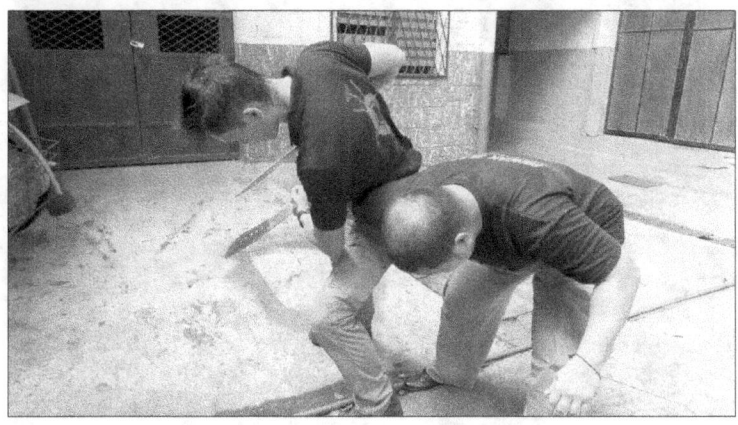

Technique 4

TECHNIQUE AGAINST A BACKHAND BODY SLASH

Threat: Your opponent swings at you with a backhand bolo slash

Response: 1) Use your blade to parry his blade with the help of your left hand to slide his blade off along yours. 2) Do this in conjunction with your footwork by stepping to your right. 3. As the assailant's blade passes by, direct the momentum of your own blade towards his face to cut him and end the encounter.

Caution: Be sure to let flat side of the blade absorb the impact in order to avoid an edge to edge impact which may reduce speed, disrupt timing, and damage your blade for further use.

Bolo vs. Bolo Techniques 109

Technique 5

TECHNIQUE AGAINST A STOMACH THRUST

Threat: Your opponent thrusts his bolo at your stomach

Response: 1) Parry the assailant's weapon downward with your left hand on top of the dull side of the bolo. 2) Simultaneously cut his arm with an upward slash of your bolo. 3) Follow up with an upward-then-downward slash to his attacking arm to finish the encounter.

Caution: Make sure to evade the thrust by moving to the side and not back pedaling along the line of attack. An assailant can move forward faster than you can move backward.

CHAPTER 10

IMPROVISED WEAPON TECHNIQUES

"Be in your Strong defense, and powerful in your offense."

— *Maestro Bong Abenir*

Most ordinary citizens and even martial artists don't carry weapons around the streets. Even those who practice Filipino martial arts and who are always practicing and drilling with sticks, swords, knives and other weapons would often rely on his arms, elbows, head butts and knees to protect themselves. This is due to the fact that carrying weapons around the streets is still illegal in most places. But to a martial artist, and especially to an eskrimador, ordinary objects could be used as a weapon, to serve as an equalizer of sorts or a shield barrier. You must use any means to survive.

Technique 1

USING A ROLLED UP MAGAZINE AGAINST A KNIFE THRUST

Threat: An assailant suddenly pulls out a knife and attacks you.

Response: 1) In this case you happen to have a magazine at hand which you could roll up and turn into an improvised weapon. 2) As the assailant thrusts his knife, step to your left side while parrying with your left hand and flick the rolled up magazine at the assailant's eyes. 3) Immediately grab his weapon hand with your left hand and break his wrist.

Caution: Remember that you have an inferior weapon at hand against an assailant who is carrying a knife. Use your weapon parry to hit his eyes with your rolled magazine. Striking it on other parts of the body might not hurt him, and may just be a waste of your energy. So go for the eyes, and make it count.

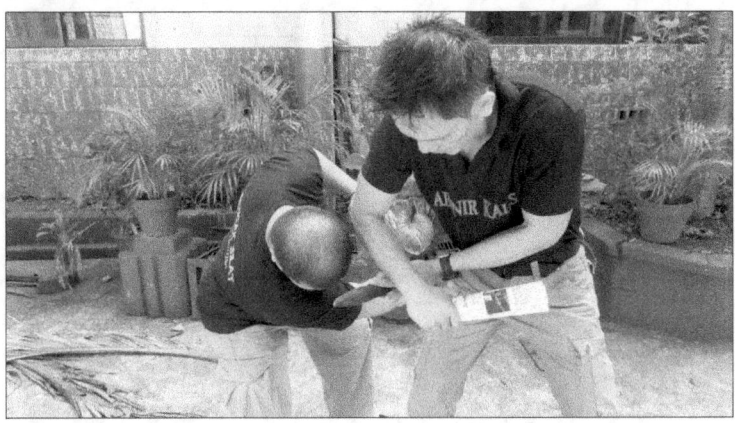

Technique 2

HARDWOOD VS. HIGH FOREHAND THRUST WITH A BROKEN BOTTLE

Threat: An assailant uses a broken bottle as a weapon to attack you

Response: 1) If you happen to see any hard object such as hard wood, or a pipe, pick it up in order to serve as an equalizer against an armed opponent. 2) As the assailant thrusts his broken bottle at you, move to the outside of his arm and strike downwards as hard as you can against his weapon hand. 3) Immediately follow up with a powerful strike to your attacker's face.

Caution: Don't be overconfident in this situation. Even though you may have a longer weapon doesn't necessarily mean your attacker won't be able to penetrate your defense. Be cautious and use your weapon to its full potential while acting quickly.

Improvised Weapon Techniques 117

Technique 3

SCARF VS. AN ICE PICK THRUST

Threat: You are confronted by an assailant wielding an ice pick

Response: 1) Step to the side and use your scarf to deflect and trap his hand by looping it around his wrist. 2) Quickly turn your body toward the assailant and loop your scarf around his neck to choke him. 3) Kick back your right leg behind his lead leg to take him down while you continue to tighten your scarf trap/choke.

Caution: Make sure that your scarf trap/hold is held tight or he might be able to maneuver out of it and continue his attack.

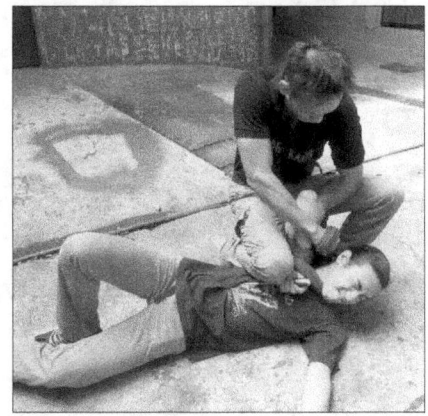

Technique 4

USING YOUR BAG AS A SHIELD AGAINST A KNIFE THRUST

Threat: An assailant lashes at you with his knife

Response: 1) If you have a bag or a back pack, you may use it as a shield against an assailant's thrusts and slash attacks. 2) If an opportunity to disarm his weapon presents itself, act on it quickly by grabbing his wrist and breaking it. 3) Maneuver in order to control him on the ground.

Caution: Use your bag to deflect and move your body away from the line of attack at the same time. Be sure to move your body together with your shield and not just rely on your hands and your bag to deflect the attack as it might penetrate and hit you.

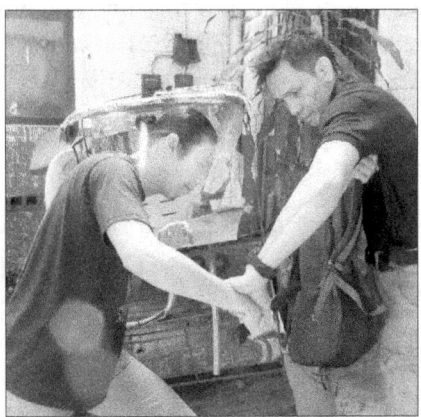
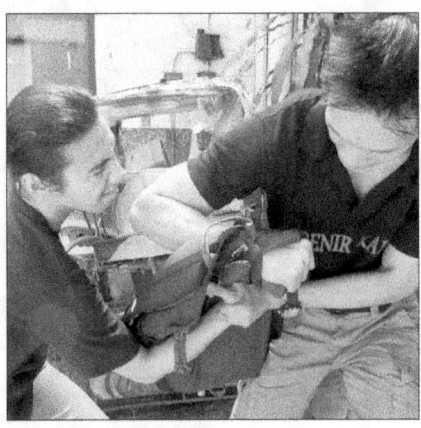
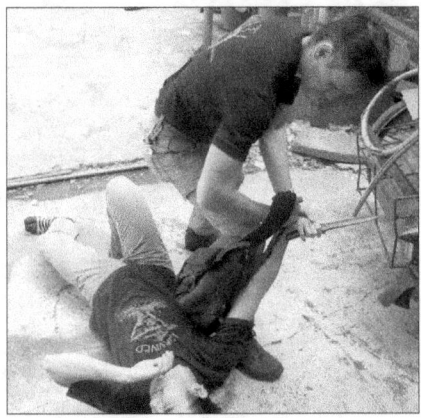

Technique 5

HARD WOOD AGAINST A BOLO ATTACK

Threat: You find yourself with an inferior weapon (such as hard wood) facing an opponent with a bolo.

Response: 1) Most bolo attacks begin with a slashing or hacking motion. Move away from the line of attack by stepping to the side and delivering a hard strike to his hands, aiming at his fingers. 2) If the result of your attack led him to release his weapon grip, immediately attack his hand again. 3) Then follow up with a smash of your weapon to his head or face.

Caution: Don't rely too much on blocking his attacks with your wood for his sharp weapon might cut through it and strike you. It is better to counter his attack by hitting him directly.

Technique 6

USING A PEN AGAINST KNIFE THRUST

Threat: You're armed with only a pen and facing an assailant with a knife

Response: 1) As the assailant thrusts his knife move to the side, parrying his weapon hand while simultaneously sweeping your pen across his eyes. 2) Immediately follow up by stabbing your pen into his ears or temple. 3) You may continue by delivering a powerful kick to the assailant's groin or thigh to take him down.

Caution: Avoid using your pen to hit hard areas of the body that might just break the pen or cause you to lose the weapon. Hit or puncture the vulnerable areas such as the eyes, throat, temple, neck and ears.

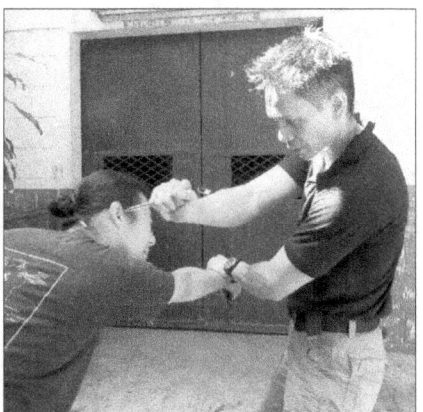

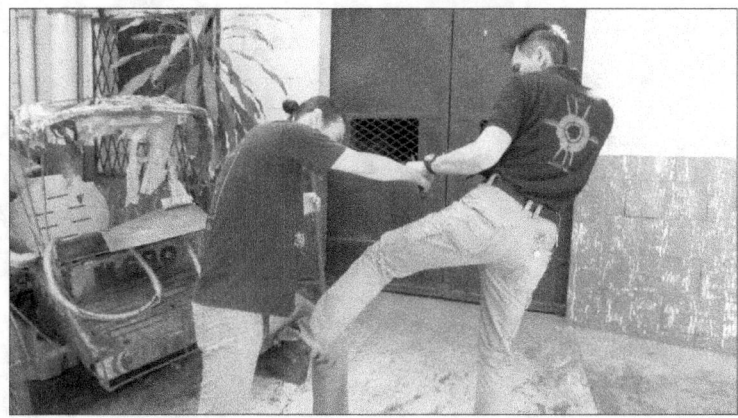

CONCLUSION

Eskrima is first and foremost a military art. This is the very reason its training begins with weapons before hand-to-hand combat. It was and still is very much a warrior's fighting art. Eskrima is always evolving and adapting, and anything that ceases to evolve and adapt is in danger of stagnation. Therefore, any true eskrimador is not afraid of change and is even ready to incorporate techniques from other systems or even foreign arts if it would enhance his fighting capability. As the saying goes, "Any means to survive is the Filipino warrior mentality."

Remember when applying a martial art for street defense—as opposed to training the art or competing in sport—simplicity is the key to success! The fastest way to connect two points is by drawing a straight line. Don't be a victim. Always present yourself as a difficult target against the enemy. Use an asymmetric attack strategy against a formidable enemy. Defeat a very strong opponent through yielding. If the enemy is trying to deceive you, pretend to be deceived. Then attack swiftly before he sees the truth. Humility can be an effective strategy. If you're up against many opponents, pull out! If he kicks your butt, smash his balls! First, attack his weak side. Then work your way up to destroy his strong side. Having a good lawyer is also a form of self-defense.

My advice to women is to learn to fight like a man. It will be a real surprise to an assailant. (Think of current MMA fighwers like Gina Carano or Ronda Rousey). Always put your strong side forward. Make your weak side strong and your strong side stronger. Don't start a fight. In a street fight, it's ok to get dirty! Fight if you must. Run if you must. Whatever you decide to do, do it quickly!

The Eskrima master is also a healer. He heals the fear of the student in handling edged and impact weapons. Once this fear has been healed the master then proceeds to heal the fear of the student when facing another human being capable of using such weapons against him. He is now able to attack and defend properly without conscious thought. All movements that were once faltering are now executed naturally. Although fear may not totally be eradicated it can properly be managed and under control. And once this is achieved the chaos involved with fear has already been healed.

ABOUT THE AUTHOR

Maestro Fernando "Bong" Abenir is a Filipino martial arts instructor based in Manila, Philippines. He started training in the martial arts at the age of 9 under the tutelage of his father in the art of kuntao. He then learned the concepts of knife fighting and surviving a street fight by a man called Mang Inyong from Masbate. This started Abenir's in-depth study in the field of martial arts at the hands of different masters and instructors. He studied Yaw-Yan under Orlando Lapuz and became an instructor under his leadership. In late 1994 he informally trained under Grand Maestro Antonio Ilustrisimo upon the introduction of Pedro Reyes but it was short-lived due to Tatang's unexpected death in 1997. Abenir continued training under Pedro Reyes and eventually was introduced to Master Tony Diego in 1998 and was granted a certificate of authorization to teach the art of Kalis Ilustrisimo. Bong Abenir was also trained in and was certified to teach Nusanatara Pencak Silat by Pendekar Mohamad Hadilmulyo, the master of Nusantara Keluarga Pencak Silat, and also from his disciple O'ong Maryono, who was a three time world Pencak Silat champion and a well-known author and researcher of the art of Silat.

In 2001 Abenir started to develop his own system until finally coming up with its name, now known as Abenir Kalis Filipino Fighting Art. Maestro Bong Abenir has also written for *Rapid Journal* and is currently a regular contributor for the *Manila Times Newspaper* in the subject of practical self-defense techniques. He has appeared in numerous TV sports and morning shows in the Philippines demonstrating his Filipino martial arts system. He has also been invited to do seminars for the Special Action Force of the Philippine National Police and has conducted seminars in the Philippines and in Queensland, Australia. Abenir is currently a physical education teacher by profession and a Filipino martial arts instructor by passion. You may contact him at abenirbong@yahoo.com or search for Bong Abenir on Facebook.

ABENIR KALIS TRAINING GROUPS

About The Author

TAMBULI MEDIA

Excellence in Mind-Body Health & Martial Arts Publishing

Welcome to Tambuli Media, publisher of quality books on mind-body martial arts and wellness presented in their cultural context.

Our Vision is to see quality books once again playing an integral role in the lives of people who pursue a journey of personal development, through the documentation and transmission of traditional knowledge of mind-body cultures.

Our Mission is to partner with the highest caliber subject-matter experts to bring you the highest quality books on important topics of health and martial arts that are in-depth, well-written, clearly illustrated and comprehensive.

Tambuli is the name of a native instrument in the Philippines fashioned from the horn of a carabao. The tambuli was blown and its sound signaled to villagers that a meeting with village elders was to be in session, or to announce the news of the day. It is hoped that Tambuli Media publications will "bring people together and disseminate the knowledge" to many.

www.TambuliMedia.com

www.ingramcontent.com/pod-product-compliance
Lightning Source LLC
Chambersburg PA
CBHW052053070526
44584CB00017B/2155